MUSICAL INSTRUMENTS

Clarinets

RUTH DALY

AV2
www.av2books.com

Step 1
Go to **www.av2books.com**

Step 2
Enter this unique code
QFNYBKJW9

Step 3
Explore your interactive eBook!

AV2 is optimized for use on any device

Your interactive eBook comes with...

- **Audio** – Listen to the entire book read aloud
- **Videos** – Watch informative video clips
- **Weblinks** – Gain additional information for research
- **Try This!** – Complete activities and hands-on experiments
- **Key Words** – Study vocabulary, and complete a matching word activity
- **Quizzes** – Test your knowledge
- **Slideshows** – View images and captions

View new titles and product videos at www.av2books.com

Clarinets Contents

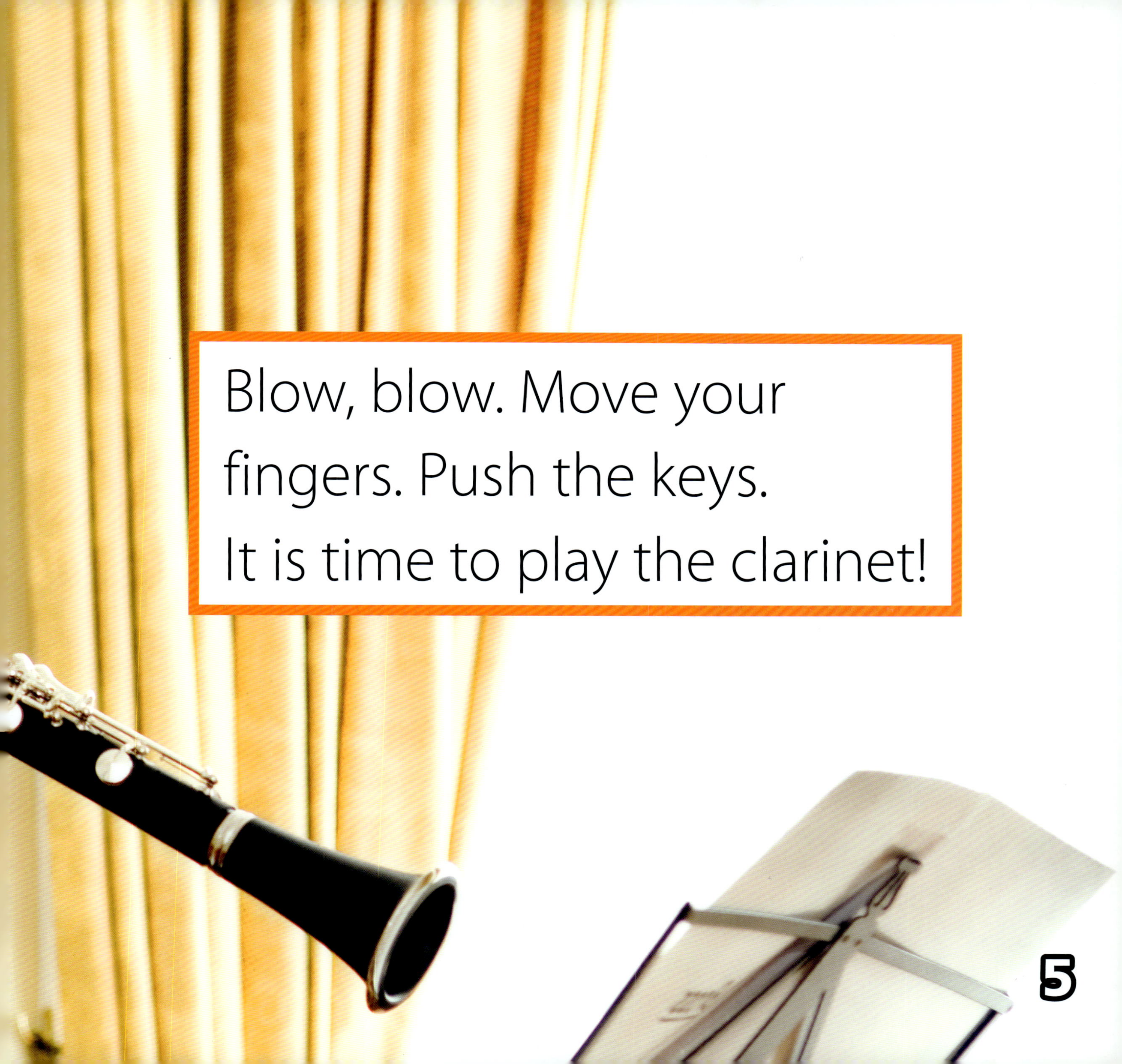

Blow, blow. Move your fingers. Push the keys. It is time to play the clarinet!

The clarinet is a kind of wind instrument. Clarinets have holes that help make sounds. Some holes are covered by pads.

Most clarinets are about 26 inches long. (66 centimeters)

A clarinet looks like a long tube. The end of the tube has a shape like a bell. It helps the clarinet make low sounds.

People blow air into the clarinet. The air moves past a piece of wood called a reed. This makes a sound.

K

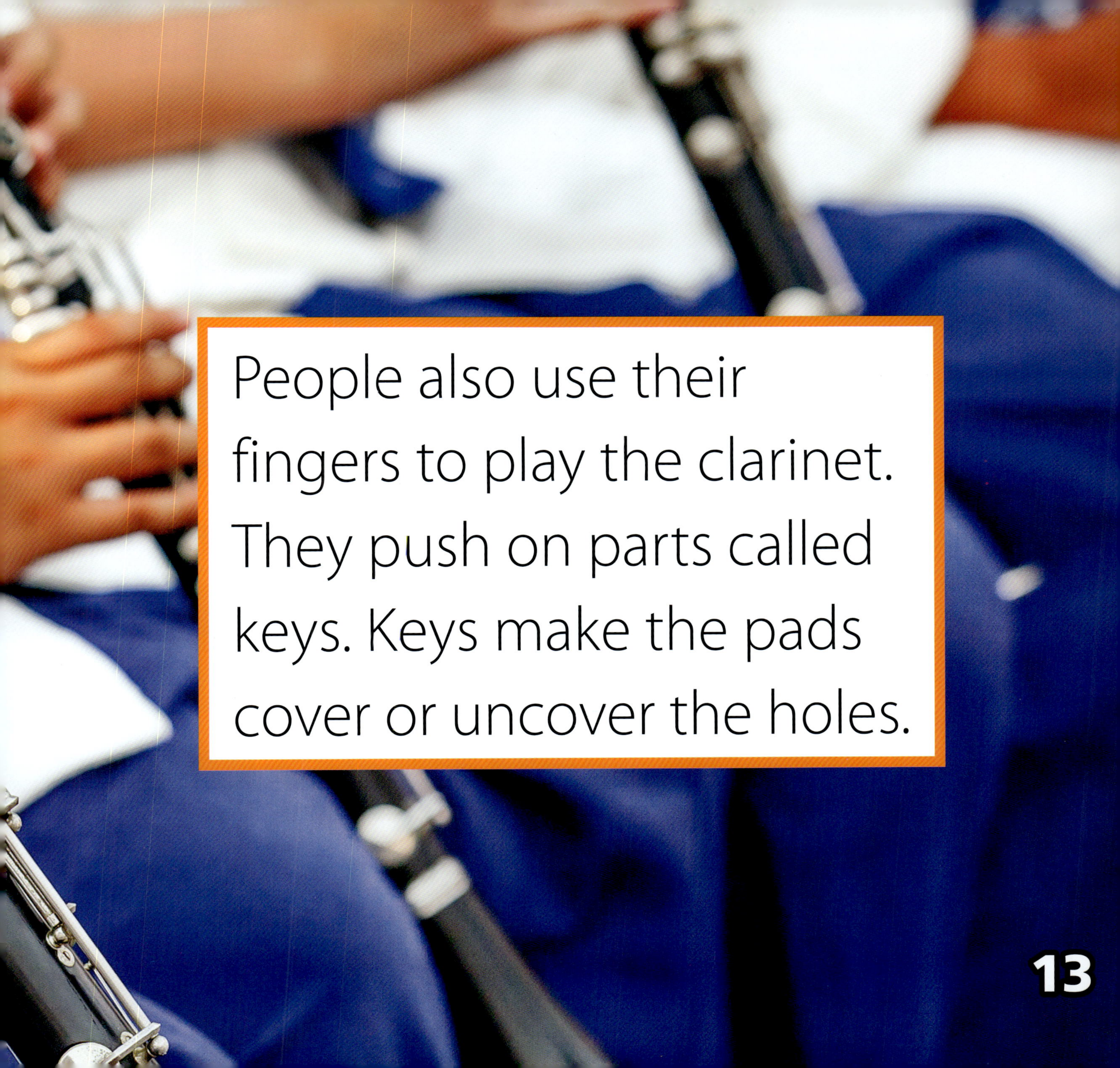

People also use their fingers to play the clarinet. They push on parts called keys. Keys make the pads cover or uncover the holes.

Clarinets are usually made of wood. They can also be plastic. The keys are covered with silver.

The clarinet was invented in Germany. Mozart wrote some of the most famous clarinet music. He was a composer who lived long ago.

The first clarinet was made about 300 years ago.

Many children play clarinets in school. These instruments are popular in school bands. Orchestras and jazz bands also have clarinets.

An orchestra usually has four clarinet players.

Clarinet players in bands also play tunes alone. This is called a solo. The song "Rhapsody in Blue" has a famous clarinet solo.

See what you have learned about clarinets.

Which of these pictures does not show a clarinet?

KEY WORDS

Research has shown that as much as 65 percent of all written material published in English is made up of 300 words. These 300 words cannot be taught using pictures or learned by sounding them out. They must be recognized by sight. This book contains 56 common sight words to help young readers improve their reading fluency and comprehension. This book also teaches young readers several important content words, such as proper nouns. These words are paired with pictures to aid in learning and improve understanding.

Page	Sight Words First Appearance
5	is, it, move, play, the, time, to, your
6	a, about, are, by, have, help, kind, long, make, most, of, some, sounds, that
9	end, has, like, looks
10	air, into, people, this
13	also, on, or, parts, their, they, use
15	be, can, made, with
16	first, he, in, lived, was, who, years
19	an, and, children, four, many, school, these
21	song

Page	Content Words First Appearance
5	clarinet, fingers, keys
6	holes, inches, pads, wind instrument
9	bell, shape, tube
10	reed, wood
15	plastic, silver
16	composer, Germany, Mozart, music
19	jazz bands, orchestras, players, school bands
21	"Rhapsody in Blue," solo, tunes

Published by AV2
350 5th Avenue, 59th Floor New York, NY 10118
Website: www.av2books.com

Library of Congress Cataloging-in-Publication Data

Names: Daly, Ruth, 1962- author.
Title: Clarinets / Ruth Daly.
Description: New York : AV2, 2020. | Series: Musical instruments |
Audience: Ages 6-9 | Audience: Grades K-1 |
Identifiers: LCCN 2019042736 (print) | LCCN 2019042737 (ebook) | ISBN 9781791116248 (library binding) |
ISBN 9781791116255 (paperback) | ISBN 9781791116262 | ISBN 9781791116279
Subjects: LCSH: Clarinet--Juvenile literature.

Classification: LCC ML945 .D35 2020 (print) | LCC ML945 (ebook) | DDC 788.6/219--dc23
LC record available at https://lccn.loc.gov/2019042736
LC ebook record available at https://lccn.loc.gov/2019042737

Printed in Guangzhou, China
1 2 3 4 5 6 7 8 9 0 24 23 22 21 20

022020
100919

Project Coordinator: John Willis Designer: Ana María Vidal

The publisher acknowledges Alamy, Getty Images, iStock, and Shutterstock as the primary image suppliers for this title.